Write Through the Bible Workbook

Philippians 2:1 - 18

ESV | Cursive

Trisha Gilkerson

IntoxicatedOnLife.com

Write Through the Bible Workbook

By: Trisha Gilkerson

Cover Design: Sarah Thomas

Intoxicated on Life • Copyright 2013 Trisha Gilkerson

Independent publishing services provided by Melinda Martin of TheHelpyHelper.com.

About *Write Through the Bible*

In 2012, while our family was memorizing Philippians 2:1-18, I was looking at what we were missing in our homeschool curriculum. I noted that I didn't have any handwriting or vocabulary work for our oldest son. I decided to create my own resource that would also help reinforce memorization of the Scripture we were working on.

If you choose to use this resource, it will integrate several subjects into one: handwriting, vocabulary, dictation, and memorization.

More Resources for Bible Memorization

It is very important for children to begin memory work from a young age. Scripture memory, specifically, is vitally important. Using this resource is not a primary means of memorization but a secondary source to reinforce Bible memorization.

If you would like more resources about Scripture-memory, you can find these resources on our blog, IntoxicatedOnLife.com:

- Free Recorded Webinar: "How to Train Your Kids to Memorize Scripture in 5 Minutes a Day" - intoxicatedonlife.com/webinar-resources/

- Memory Time Freebies: Make your own Charlotte-Mason-style memory box and print free Scripture cards - intoxicatedonlife.com/freebies/

- How to Use Copywork for Bible Memorization - intoxicatedonlife.com/2013/03/09/copywork-for-bible-memorization/

- 5 Great Ideas to Help Your Choose Bible Memory Verses for Kids - intoxicatedonlife.com/2013/04/01/bible-memory-verses-for-kids-choosin/

- Blog Posts about Memory Work: Read the latest posts of Bible memory ideas - intoxicatedonlife.com/category/memory-work/

How to Use this Resource

For a typical school year, you will need to use this workbook 4 days each week to complete all exercises.

This resource is fully adaptable to your situation. If the selections are too long, shorten them. If the paper does not have the correct sized lines, use your own paper.

- The first 3 days your child will copy a short passage.

- The next 1-2 days your child will look up vocabulary words and write definitions.

- The next day you will dictate the passage to your child to write out as you speak.

- The next several days your child will copy that last 3 sections together.

Tips for Parents

- Encourage your child to focus on neatness and using their very best handwriting

- Be sure to go over their work and praise them for good handwriting and correct where necessary.

- There may be times your child needs help choosing the best definition to fit their vocabulary word. There are often many different choices, depending on the dictionary used. Do give assistance where it is needed and help your child think through the possibilities.

Extra Resources in the Back

You will find an appendix at the end of this document. It contains three resources to assist you:

- The complete portion of Scripture being used in this resource, broken into the segments being used throughout the book

- Each of the vocabulary words with appropriate definitions (note, these are not the only definitions that can be used)

- Extra paper you may copy in case your child runs out of room

Share Your Work

We would love for you to share your child's work with us. E-mail a picture of their work to intoxicatedonlifemail@gmail.com. Please, let us know what you think of this workbook!

Day 1: Copy Verse

Philippians 2:1

So if there is any encouragement in

Christ, any comfort from love, any

participation in the Spirit, any affection

and sympathy,

Day 2: Copy Verse

Philippians 2:1

So if there is any encouragement in

Christ, any comfort from love, any

participation in the Spirit, any affection

and sympathy,

Day 3: Copy Verse

Philippians 2:1

So if there is any encouragement in

Christ, any comfort from love, any

participation in the Spirit, any affection

and sympathy,

Day 4: Vocabulary

Encouragement:

Comfort:

Participation:

Day 5: Vocabulary

Affection:

Sympathy:

Day 6: Dictation

Philippians 2:1

Day 7: Copy Verse

Philippians 2:2

complete my joy by being of the same

mind, having the same love, being in

full accord and of one mind.

Day 8: Copy Verse

Philippians 2:2

complete my joy by being of the same

mind, having the same love, being in

full accord and of one mind.

Day 9: Copy Verse

Philippians 2:2

complete my joy by being of the same

mind, having the same love, being in

full accord and of one mind.

Day 10: Vocabulary

Joy:

Accord:

Day 11: Dictation

Philippians 2:2

Days 12 & 13: Copy Verses

Philippians 2:1-2

So if there is any encouragement in

Christ, any comfort from love, any

participation in the Spirit, any affection

and sympathy, complete my joy by

being of the same mind, having the same

love, being in full accord and of one

mind.

Day 14: Copy Verse

Philippians 2:3

Do nothing from selfish ambition or conceit, but in humility count others more significant than yourselves.

Day 15: Copy Verse

Philippians 2:3

Do nothing from selfish ambition or

conceit, but in humility count others

more significant than yourselves.

Day 16: Copy Verse

Philippians 2:3

Do nothing from selfish ambition or

conceit, but in humility count others

more significant than yourselves.

Day 17: Vocabulary

Ambition:

Conceit:

Day 18: Vocabulary

Humility:

Significant:

Day 19: Dictation

Philippians 2:3

Days 20 - 22: Copy Verses

Philippians 2:1-3

So if there is any encouragement in

Christ, any comfort from love, any

participation in the Spirit, any affection

and sympathy, complete my joy by

being of the same mind, having the same

love, being in full accord and of one

mind. Do nothing from selfish ambition

or conceit, but in humility count others

Days 20 - 22: Copy Verses

Philippians 2:1-3 (continued)

more significant than yourselves.

Day 23: Copy Verse

Philippians 2:4-5

Let each of you look not only to his own

interests, but also to the interests of others.

Have this mind among yourselves, which

is yours in Christ Jesus,

Day 24: Copy Verse

Philippians 2:4-5

Let each of you look not only to his own
interests, but also to the interests of others.
Have this mind among yourselves, which
is yours in Christ Jesus,

Day 25: Copy Verse

Philippians 2:4-5

Let each of you look not only to his own

interests, but also to the interests of others.

Have this mind among yourselves, which

is yours in Christ Jesus,

Day 26: Vocabulary

Interests:

Mind:

Day 27: Dictation

Philippians 2:4-5

Days 28 - 30: Copy Verses

Philippians 2:2-5

complete my joy by being of the same

mind, having the same love, being in

full accord and of one mind. Do nothing

from selfish ambition or conceit, but in

humility count others more significant

than yourselves. Let each of you look not

only to his own interests, but also to the

interests of others. Have this mind among

Days 28 - 30: Copy Verses

Philippians 2:2-5 (continued)

yourselves, which is yours in Christ Jesus,

Day 31: Copy Verse

Philippians 2:6

who, though he was in the form of God,

did not count equality with God a thing

to be grasped,

Day 32: Copy Verse

Philippians 2:6

who, though he was in the form of God,

did not count equality with God a thing

to be grasped,

Day 33: Copy Verse

Philippians 2:6

who, though he was in the form of God,

did not count equality with God a thing

to be grasped,

Day 34: Vocabulary

Form:

Equality:

Grasp:

Day 35: Dictation

Philippians 2:6

Days 36 - 38: Copy Verses

Philippians 2:3-6

Do nothing from selfish ambition or

conceit, but in humility count others

more significant than yourselves. Let

each of you look not only to his own

interests, but also to the interests of others.

Have this mind among yourselves, which

is yours in Christ Jesus, who, though he

was in the form of God, did not count

Days 36 – 38: Copy Verses

Philippians 2:3-6 (continued)

equality with God a thing to be grasped,

Day 39: Copy Verse

Philippians 2:7

but emptied himself, by taking the form

of a servant, being born in the likeness

of men.

Day 40: Copy Verse

Philippians 2:7

but emptied himself, by taking the form

of a servant, being born in the likeness

of men.

Day 41: Copy Verse

Philippians 2:7

but emptied himself, by taking the form

of a servant, being born in the likeness

of men.

Day 42: Vocabulary

Likeness:

Servant:

Day 43: Dictation

Philippians 2:7

Days 44 – 46: Copy Verses

Philippians 2:4-7

Let each of you look not only to his own

interests, but also to the interests of others.

Have this mind among yourselves, which

is yours in Christ Jesus, who, though he

was in the form of God, did not count

equality with God a thing to be grasped,

but emptied himself, by taking the form

of a servant, being born in the likeness

Days 44 - 46: Copy Verses

Philippians 2:4-7 (continued)

of men.

Day 47: Copy Verse

Philippians 2:8

And being found in human form, he

humbled himself by becoming obedient to

the point of death, even death on a cross.

Day 48: Copy Verse

Philippians 2:8

And being found in human form, he

humbled himself by becoming obedient to

the point of death, even death on a cross.

Day 49: Copy Verse

Philippians 2:8

And being found in human form, he

humbled himself by becoming obedient to

the point of death, even death on a cross.

Day 50: Vocabulary

Humbled:

Obedient:

Day 51: Dictation

Philippians 2:8

Days 52 - 54: Copy Verses

Philippians 2:6-8

who, though he was in the form of God,

did not count equality with God a thing

to be grasped, but emptied himself, by

taking the form of a servant, being born

in the likeness of men. And being found

in human form, he humbled himself by

becoming obedient to the point of death,

even death on a cross.

Day 55: Copy Verse

Philippians 2:9

Therefore God has highly exalted him and

bestowed on him the name that is above

every name,

Day 56: Copy Verse

Philippians 2:9

Therefore God has highly exalted him and

bestowed on him the name that is above

every name,

Day 57: Copy Verse

Philippians 2:9

Therefore God has highly exalted him and

bestowed on him the name that is above

every name,

Day 58: Vocabulary

Exalted:

Bestowed:

Day 59: Dictation

Philippians 2:9

Days 60 - 62: Copy Verses

Philippians 2:7-9

but emptied himself, by taking the form

of a servant, being born in the likeness

of men. And being found in human

form, he humbled himself by becoming

obedient to the point of death, even death

on a cross. Therefore God has highly exalted

him and bestowed on him the name that

is above every name,

Day 63: Copy Verse

Philippians 2:10

so that at the name of Jesus every knee

should bow, in heaven and on the earth

and under the earth,

Day 64: Copy Verse

Philippians 2:10

so that at the name of Jesus every knee

should bow, in heaven and on the earth

and under the earth,

Day 65: Copy Verse

Philippians 2:10

so that at the name of Jesus every knee

should bow, in heaven and on the earth

and under the earth,

Day 66: Vocabulary

Bow:

Heaven:

Day 67: Dictation

Philippians 2:10

Days 68 - 70: Copy Verses

Philippians 2:8-10

And being found in human form, he

humbled himself by becoming obedient to

the point of death, even death on a cross.

Therefore God has highly exalted him and

bestowed on him the name that is above

every name, so that at the name of Jesus

every knee should bow, in heaven and on

earth and under the earth,

Day 71: Copy Verse

Philippians 2:11

and every tongue confess that Jesus Christ

is Lord, to the glory of God the Father

Day 72: Copy Verse

Philippians 2:11

and every tongue confess that Jesus Christ

is Lord, to the glory of God the Father

Day 73: Copy Verse

Philippians 2:11

and every tongue confess that Jesus Christ

is Lord, to the glory of God the Father

Day 74: Vocabulary

Confess:

Glory:

Day 75: Dictation

Philippians 2:11

Days 76 - 78: Copy Verses

Philippians 2:9-11

Therefore God has highly exalted him and

bestowed on him the name that is above

every name, so that at the name of Jesus

every knee should bow, in heaven and

on earth and under the earth, and every

tongue confess that Jesus Christ is Lord, to

the glory of God the Father.

Day 79: Copy Verse

Philippians 2:12a

Therefore, my beloved, as you have always

obeyed, so now, not only as in my

presence but much more in my absence,

Day 80: Copy Verse

Philippians 2:12a

Therefore, my beloved, as you have always

obeyed, so now, not only as in my

presence but much more in my absence,

Day 81: Copy Verse

Philippians 2:12a

Therefore, my beloved, as you have always

obeyed, so now, not only as in my

presence but much more in my absence,

Day 82: Vocabulary

Obey:

Presence:

Absence:

Day 83: Dictation

Philippians 2:12a

Days 84 - 86: Copy Verses

Philippians 2:10-12a

so that at the name of Jesus every knee

should bow, in heaven and on earth and

under the earth, and every tongue confess

that Jesus Christ is Lord, to the glory of

God the Father. Therefore, my beloved, as

you have always obeyed, so now, not

only as in my presence but much more

in my absence,

Day 87: Copy Verse

Philippians 2:12b-13

work out your own salvation with fear

and trembling, for it is God who works

in you, both to will and to work for his

good pleasure.

Day 88: Copy Verse

Philippians 2:12b-13

work out your own salvation with fear

and trembling, for it is God who works

in you, both to will and to work for his

good pleasure.

Day 89: Copy Verse

Philippians 2:12b-13

work out your own salvation with fear

and trembling, for it is God who works

in you, both to will and to work for his

good pleasure.

Day 90: Vocabulary

Trembling:

Pleasure:

Day 91: Dictation

Philippians 2:12b-13

Days 92 - 94: Copy Verses

Philippians 2:11-13

and every tongue confess that Jesus Christ

is Lord, to the glory of God the Father.

Therefore, my beloved, as you have always

obeyed, so now, not only as in my

presence but much more in my absence,

work out your own salvation with fear

and trembling, for it is God who works

in you, both to will and to work for his

Days 92 - 94: Copy Verses

Philippians 2:11-13 (continued)

good pleasure.

Day 95: Copy Verse

Philippians 2:14 - 15a

Do all things without grumbling or

disputing, that you may be blameless and

innocent,

Day 96: Copy Verse

Philippians 2:14 - 15a

Do all things without grumbling or

disputing, that you many be blameless and

innocent,

Day 97: Copy Verse

Philippians 2:14 - 15a

Do all things without grumbling or

disputing, that you may be blameless and

innocent,

Day 98: Vocabulary

Grumbling:

Disputing:

Day 99: Vocabulary

Blameless:

Innocent:

Day 100: Dictation

Philippians 2:14-15a

Days 101 - 103: Copy Verses

Philippians 2:12-15a

Therefore, my beloved, as you have always

obeyed, so now, not only as in my

presence but much more in my absence,

work out your own salvation with fear

and trembling, for it is God who works

in you, both to will and to work for

his good pleasure. Do all things without

grumbling or disputing, that you may be

Days 101 – 103: Copy Verses

Philippians 2:12-15a (continued)

blameless and innocent,

Day 104: Copy Verse

Philippians 2:15b

children of God without blemish in the

midst of a crooked and twisted generation,

among whom you shine as lights in the

world,

Day 105: Copy Verse

Philippians 2:15b

children of God without blemish in the

midst of a crooked and twisted generation,

among whom you shine as lights in the

world,

Day 106: Copy Verse

Philippians 2:15b

children of God without blemish in the

midst of a crooked and twisted generation,

among whom you shine as lights in the

world,

Day 107: Vocabulary

Crooked:

Generation:

Day 108: Dictation

Philippians 2:15b

Days 109 - 111: Copy Verses

Philippians 2:12b-15

work out your own salvation with fear

and trembling, for it is God who works

in you, both to will and to work for

his good pleasure. Do all things without

grumbling or disputing, that you may be

blameless and innocent, children of God

without blemish in the midst of a crooked

and twisted generation, among whom you

Days 109 - 111: Copy Verses

Philippians 2:12b-15 (continued)

shine as lights in the world,

Day 112: Copy Verse

Philippians 2:16

holding fast to the word of life, so that

in the day of Christ I may be proud

that I did not run in vain or labor in

vain.

Day 113: Copy Verse

Philippians 2:16

holding fast to the word of life, so that

in the day of Christ I may be proud

that I did not run in vain or labor in

vain.

Day 114: Copy Verse

Philippians 2:16

holding fast to the word of life, so that

in the day of Christ I may be proud

that I did not run in vain or labor in

vain.

Day 115: Vocabulary

Proud:

Vain:

Day 116: Dictation

Philippians 2:16

Days 117 - 119: Copy Verses

Philippians 2:14-16

Do all things without grumbling or

disputing, that you may be blameless and

innocent, children of God without blemish

in the midst of a crooked and twisted

generation, among whom you shine as

lights in the world, holding fast to the

word of life, so that in the day of Christ

I may be proud that I did not run in

Days 117 - 119: Copy Verses

Philippians 2:14-16 (continued)

vain or labor in vain.

Day 120: Copy Verse

Philippians 2:17

Even if I am to be poured out as a

drink offering upon the sacrificial offering

of your faith, I am glad and rejoice with

you all.

206 | IntoxicatedOnLife.com

Day 121: Copy Verse

Philippians 2:17

Even if I am to be poured out as a

drink offering upon the sacrificial offering

of your faith, I am glad and rejoice with

you all.

Day 122: Copy Verse

Philippians 2:17

Even if I am to be poured out as a

drink offering upon the sacrificial offering

of your faith, I am glad and rejoice with

you all.

Day 123: Vocabulary

Offering:

Sacrificial:

Day 124: Dictation

Philippians 2:17

Days 125 - 127: Copy Verses

Philippians 2:15b-17

children of God without blemish in the

midst of a crooked and twisted generation,

among whom you shine as lights in the

world, holding fast to the word of life, so

that in the day of Christ I may be proud

that I did not run in vain or labor in

vain. Even if I am to be poured out as a

drink offering upon the sacrificial offering

Days 125 - 127: Copy Verses

Philippians 2:15b-17 (continued)

of your faith, I am glad and rejoice with

you all.

Day 128: Copy Verse

Philippians 2:18

Likewise you also should be glad and

rejoice with me.

Day 129: Copy Verse

Philippians 2:18

Likewise you also should be glad and

rejoice with me.

Day 130: Copy Verse

Philippians 2:18

Likewise you also should be glad and
rejoice with me.

Day 131: Vocabulary

Likewise:

Rejoice:

Day 132: Dictation

Philippians 2:18

Days 133 - 135: Copy Verses

Philippians 2:16-18

holding fast to the word of life, so that

in the day of Christ I may be proud

that I did not run in vain or labor in

vain. Even if I am to be poured out as a

drink offering upon the sacrificial offering

of your faith, I am glad and rejoice with

you all. Likewise you also should be glad

and rejoice with me.

Appendix A: Philippians 2:1-18

The following is Philippians 2:1-18 divided up as it is for your child through this resource.

1   So if there is any encouragement in Christ, any comfort from love, any participation in the Spirit, any affection and sympathy,

2   complete my joy by being of the same mind, having the same love, being in full accord and of one mind.

3   Do nothing from selfish ambition or conceit, but in humility count others more significant than yourselves.

4   Let each of you look not only to his own interests, but also to the interests of others. 5 Have this mind among yourselves, which is yours in Christ Jesus,

6   who, though he was in the form of God, did not count equality with God a thing to be grasped,

7   but emptied himself, by taking the form of a servant, being born in the likeness of men.

8   And being found in human form, he humbled himself by becoming obedient to the point of death, even death on a cross.

9   Therefore God has highly exalted him and bestowed on him the name that is above every name,

10   so that at the name of Jesus every knee should bow, in heaven and on earth and under the earth,

11   and every tongue confess that Jesus Christ is Lord, to the glory of God the Father.

12a   Therefore, my beloved, as you have always obeyed, so now, not only as in my presence but much more in my absence,

12b   work out your own salvation with fear and trembling, 13 for it is God who works in you, both to will and to work for his good pleasure.

14   Do all things without grumbling or disputing, 15a that you may be blameless and innocent,

15b   children of God without blemish in the midst of a crooked and twisted generation, among whom you shine as lights in the world,

16   holding fast to the word of life, so that in the day of Christ I may be proud that I did

not run in vain or labor in vain.

17   Even if I am to be poured out as a drink offering upon the sacrificial offering of your faith, I am glad and rejoice with you all.

18   Likewise you also should be glad and rejoice with me.

Appendix B: Vocabulary Words & Definitions

Below are all of the vocabulary words that are found throughout this workbook along with definitions. Please be aware these are only a list of possible definitions.

Absence: The state of being away, or not being present

Accord: To be in agreement or harmony

Affection: Fond attachment, affection, or love

Ambition: A strong desire for success

Bestowed: To present as a gift

Blameless: Free from guilt, not deserving blame

Bowed: To bend the knee or body in reverence or submission

Comfort: To soothe, console, or reassure

Conceit: Having an excessively favorable opinion of oneself

Confess: To acknowledge one's belief or faith in

Crooked: Not straightforward, dishonest

Disputing: To engage in argument

Encouragement: To inspire with courage and confidence

Equality: The state of being equal

Exalted: Raised or elevated in rank or character

Form: The shape of a thing or person

Generation: Belonging to a certain phase of life

Glory: Very great praise, honor

Grasp: To seize upon and hold firmly

Grumbling: To murmur or mutter discontentedly; to complain

Heaven: The abode of God and the angels

Humbled: Low in rank, importance, or status

Humility: Having a modest opinion of oneself

Innocent: Being without sin

Interests: To the benefit or advantage of one

Joy: The emotion of great delight or happiness

Likeness: The semblance or appearance of

Likewise: In like manner

Mind: To have an understanding

Obedient: Willing to obey or be compliant

Obey: To comply with or follow commands

Offering: A contribution given in worship or devotion

Participation: To be actively involved in

Pleasure: Enjoyment or satisfaction

Presence: Being in attendance

Proud: Having pleasure or satisfaction over something regarded as honorable

Rejoice: Be glad

Sacrificial: Pertaining to a sacrifice

Servant: A person in the service of another

Significant: Important or notable

Sympathy: The sharing of another's emotions

Trembling: To be apprehensive

Vain: Something that is unsuccessful

More *Write Through the Bible* Copywork Workbooks

Purchase more copywork printables at IntoxicatedOnLife.com. Currently we have several passages available in both English Standard Version and the King James Version. We also have cursive and manuscript versions for all our books.

See all our available books:

intoxicatedonlife.com/copywork-printables-write-through-the-bible/

Have a suggestion or question? Let us know!

intoxicatedonlife.com/copywork-printables-write-through-the-bible/comments-and-suggestions/

Accompanying Bible Studies

Don't stop with just Scripture memory! We have a growing list of family Bible studies that work hand-in-hand with our *Write Through the Bible* handwriting workbooks. These 30-day studies will help your whole family grasp the significance of these famous Bible passages.

intoxicatedonlife.com/welcome-store/

Made in the USA
Lexington, KY
28 March 2015